Strategic Paper P3
Risk Management

Second edition 2015

ISBN 9781 4727 3438 9
e ISBN 9781 4727 3660 4

British Library Cataloguing-in-Publication Data
A catalogue record for this book is available from the
British Library

Published by

BPP Learning Media Ltd,
BPP House, Aldine Place,
142-144 Uxbridge Road,
London W12 8AA

www.bpp.com/learningmedia

Printed in the United Kingdom

Welcome to BPP Learning Media's CIMA **Passcards** for **Strategic Paper P3 Risk Management**.

- They **focus on your exam** and **save you time**.

- They incorporate **diagrams** to kick start your memory.

- They follow the overall **structure** of the BPP Learning Media Study Texts, but BPP Learning Media's CIMA **Passcards** are not just a condensed book. Each card has been separately designed for clear presentation. Topics are self contained and can be grasped visually.

- CIMA **Passcards** are still **just the right size** for pockets, briefcases and bags.

Run through the **Passcards** as often as you can during your final revision period. The day before the exam, try to go through the **Passcards** again! You will then be well on your way to passing your exams.

Good luck!

Contents

1: Introduction to risk

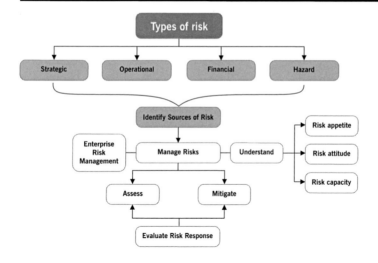

Risk

is a condition in which there exists a quantifiable dispersion in the possible outcomes from any activity. Risk can be classified in a number of ways.

Risk classification

Fundamental risks	Affect society in general and cannot be controlled by one individual
Particular risks	Risks over which individuals may have some control
Speculative risks	Risks from which either good or harm may result
Pure risks	Risks whose only possible outcome is harmful

Uncertainty

Uncertainty means possible outcomes and/or chances of each occurring are unknown.

Risk and return

Businesses/shareholders may tolerate higher risk levels provided they can receive a higher return.

Benefits of risk management

- Predictability of cash flows
- Well-run systems
- Limitation of impact of potentially bankrupting events
- Increased shareholder and investor confidence

Risk drivers

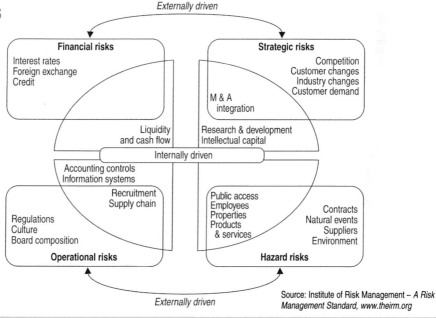

Externally driven

Financial risks

Interest rates
Foreign exchange
Credit

Strategic risks

Competition
Customer changes
Industry changes
Customer demand

M & A
integration

Liquidity
and cash flow

Research & development
Intellectual capital

Internally driven

Accounting controls
Information systems

Recruitment
Supply chain

Public access
Employees
Properties
Products
& services

Contracts
Natural events
Suppliers
Environment

Regulations
Culture
Board composition

Operational risks

Hazard risks

Externally driven

Source: Institute of Risk Management – *A Risk Management Standard*, www.theirm.org

Strategic risk

is the potential volatility of profits caused by the nature and type of business operations.

Strategic risks

Business risks

Non-business risks

Competitor action

Product obsolescence

New technology

Finance

Accident/ disaster

| Nature of risks | Strategic risks | Operational risks | Financial and hazard | Risk management models | Risk appetite and aptitude | Risk assessment | Risk mitigation |

Operational risk

is the risk of loss from a failure of internal business and control processes. It is also known as **process risk**.

1: Introduction to risk

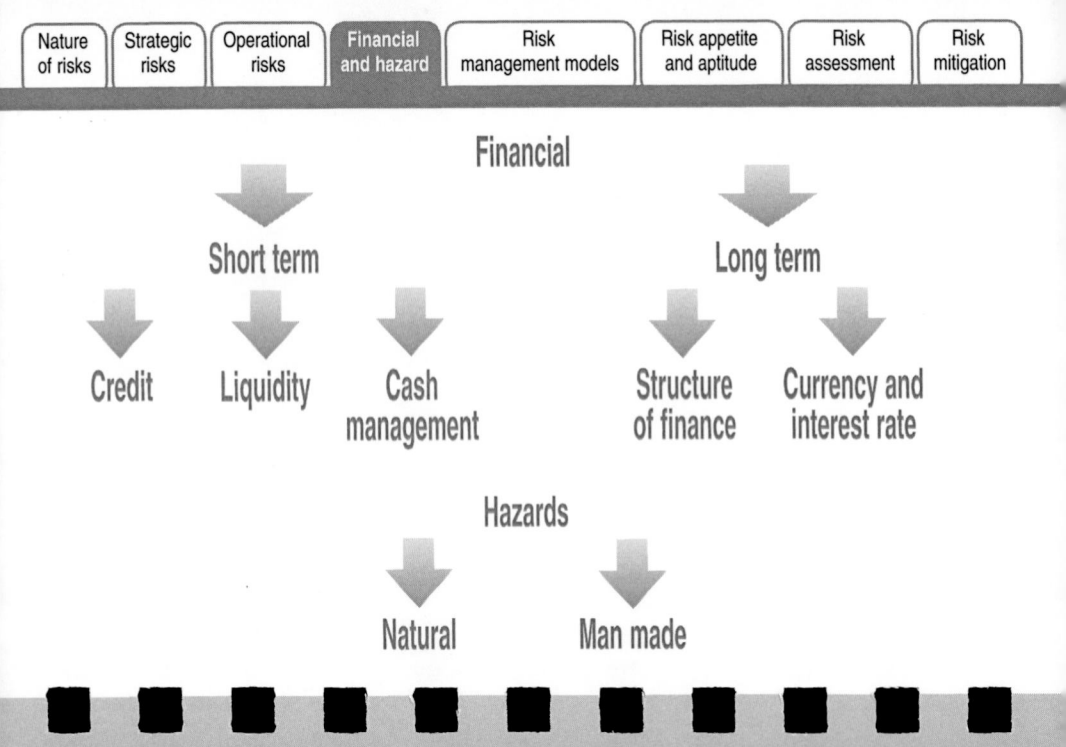

Financial

Short term

Long term

Credit

Liquidity

Cash management

Structure of finance

Currency and interest rate

Hazards

Natural

Man made

| Nature of risks | Strategic risks | Operational risks | Financial and hazard | **Risk management models** | Risk appetite and aptitude | Risk assessment | Risk mitigation |

Enterprise risk management (ERM)

is a process effected by the board of directors, management and other personnel, applied in strategy setting and across the enterprise, to identify potential events that may affect the entity and to manage risks to be within its risk appetite, and to provide reasonable assurance regarding the achievement of objectives.

ERM characteristics

- Process
- Operated at every level
- Applied in strategy setting
- Applied across enterprise

- Identifies key risks and manages the risk
- Provides reasonable assurance
- Geared to achievement of objectives

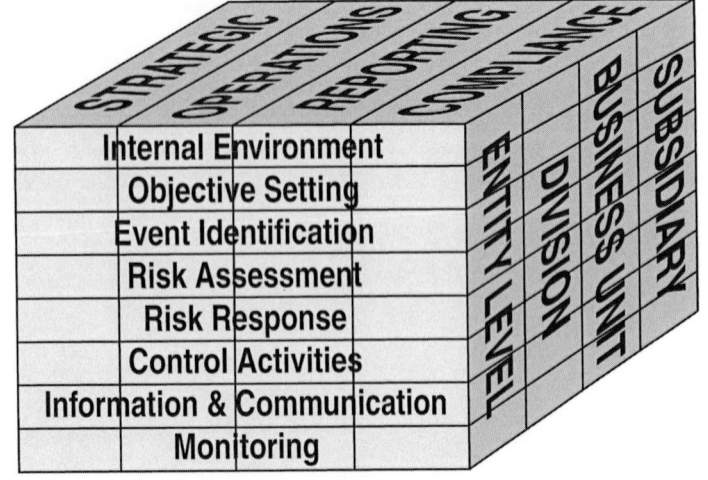

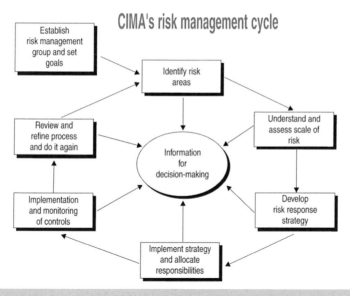

CIMA's risk management cycle

- Establish risk management group and set goals
- Identify risk areas
- Understand and assess scale of risk
- Develop risk response strategy
- Implement strategy and allocate responsibilities
- Implementation and monitoring of controls
- Review and refine process and do it again

Information for decision-making

IFAC's Risk architecture

The risk architecture involves designing and implementing organisational structures, systems and processes to manage risk. It is slightly different to ERM.

Risk architecture components

- Acceptance of a risk management framework
- Commitment from executives
- Establishment of a risk response strategy
- Assignment of responsibility
- Resourcing
- Communication and training
- Reinforcing risk cultures
- Monitoring

IFAC's components of risk management

1 Structure

2 Resources

3 Culture

4 Tools and techniques

| Nature of risks | Strategic risks | Operational risks | Financial and hazard | Risk management models | Risk appetite and aptitude | Risk assessment | Risk mitigation |

Personal views

Shareholder demands

Influences on risk appetite

Cultural influences

National influences

Organisational influences

Risk viewpoints

- Fatalists
- Hierarchists
- Individuals
- Egalitarians

Conformance and Performance

Conformance – Focus on controlling strategic risks by regulations, best practice, fiduciary responsibilities, efficient + effective risk management

Performance – Taking opportunities to increase returns, by alignment of strategy, value creation + resource utilisation

- Event identification
- Inspection of physical conditions/documents
- Enquiries and brainstorming
- Checklists
- Benchmarking
- Human reliability analysis

Identification

- Average results
- Frequency/chances of losses
- Largest possible loss

Analysis

Risk assessment

Mapping

Grouping risks into risk families, based on

- Frequency/likelihood
- Severity/consequences

Consolidation

- Aggregate of subsidiary risks for whole organisation

Dealing with risk

			Severity

Abandonment	Not investing in high risk/high cost operations
Reduce	Contingency planning, physical measures (alarms, fire precautions) awareness and commitment
Acceptance	Bear full cost if risk materialises; valid if risks insignificant or avoidance costs too great
Transfer	To suppliers, customers, insurers, state
Sharing	With insurers/joint venture partners
Diversification	Portfolio management
Hedging	Incurring risks in opposite direction

		Severity	
		LOW	HIGH
Frequency	LOW	Accept	Transfer
	HIGH	Reduce	Avoid

1: Introduction to risk

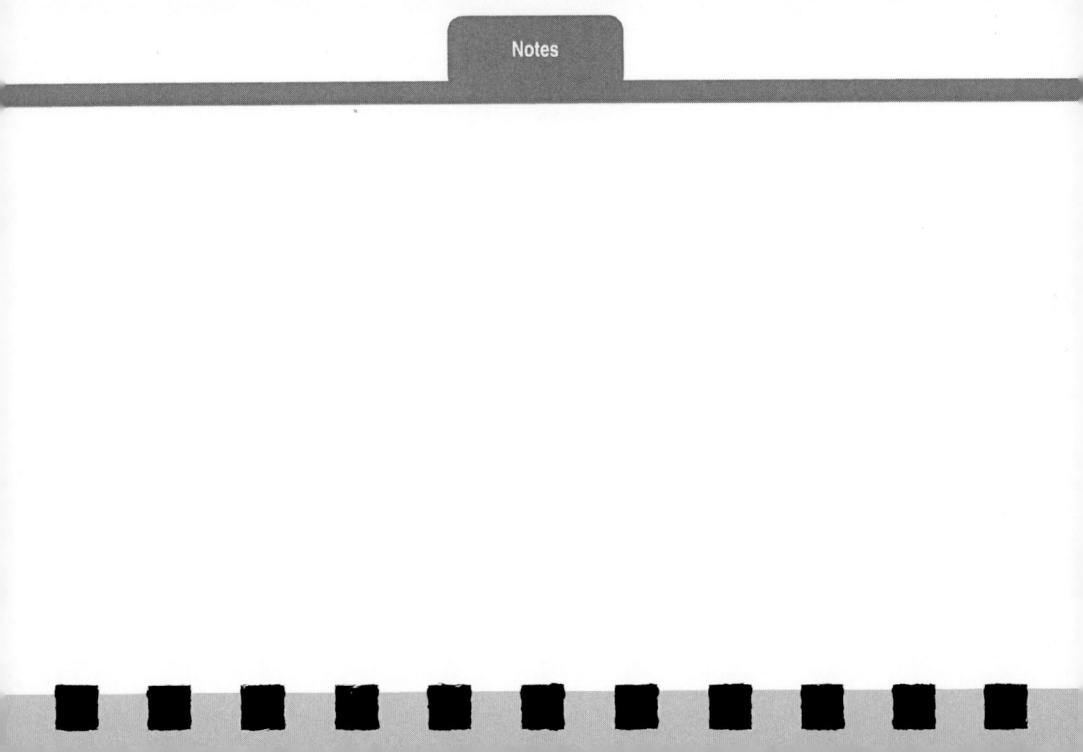

Notes

2: Governance

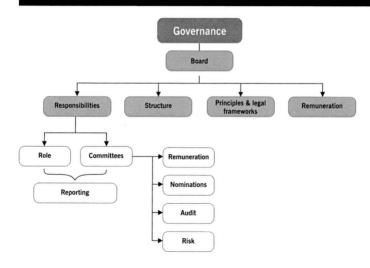

Corporate governance

is the system by which organisations are directed and controlled.

Poor corporate governance

- Domination by single individual
- Lack of board involvement
- Lack of internal controls/audit
- Poor supervision
- No independent scrutiny
- Little contact with shareholders
- Short-term profits all important
- Misleading accounts

Governance principles

- Adhere to strategic objectives
- Minimise risk
- Promote integrity
- Fulfil responsibilities to stakeholders
- Establish accountability
- Maintain auditor/non-executive independence
- Report accurately and promptly
- Encourage shareholder involvement

Corporate governance reports

UK

- UK Corporate Governance Code
- Turnbull (internal control)
- Smith (audit committees)
- Higgs (non-executive directors)

USA

- Sarbanes – Oxley Act 2002

OECD

- Principles of corporate governance

Principles vs rules

A continuing debate on corporate governance is whether the guidance should predominantly be in the form of principles, or whether there is a detailed need for laws or regulations.

Directors' abilities and performance

- Relevant expertise
- Mix of experience/diversity on board
- Appropriate training
- Assess board performance at least once a year

Role of board

- Develop and ensure implementation of strategy
- Take major decisions (mergers, asset acquisitions, financing)
- Oversee chief executive
- Monitor risks and control systems
- Monitor human capital
- Oversee communication

Board membership

A nomination committee should oversee appointment process and make recommendations to the board, using objective criteria but attempting to recruit from a wide field.

Division of responsibilities

Effective power should not be vested in one person.

- Separation of chairman and chief executive
- Non-executive directors
- Senior independent director(s)

Chairman and Chief executive

Chairman runs board, responsible for shareholder communication and ensuring board has accurate data.

Chief executive oversees strategy, runs operations and control systems.

Non-executive directors (NEDs)

- No executive (managerial) responsibilities
- Provide balance
- Help reduce conflict
- Majority should be independent (no business/financial connection, no share options/pensions)

Role of NEDs

- Strategy
- Scrutiny
- Risk management
- Board personnel

NEDs

Advantages
- External experience and knowledge
- Wider perspective
- Comfort for investors
- Confidant/enabler
- Board members but objective

Disadvantages
- Independence?
- Restricted recruitment
- Difficult to impose views
- Can't prevent problems
- Limited time

2: Governance

Principles

UK guidance suggests:

- Directors' remuneration set by independent board members
- Bonuses/performance related pay related to measurable performance/enhanced shareholder value/long-term interests of company
- Full transparency in annual accounts

Remuneration committee

Committee of independent NEDs determining:

- Remuneration policy
- Specific remuneration packages

Should consider need to attract directors, interests of stakeholders, weighting and phasing of different parts of package including share options, performance measures.

Remuneration statement

Consider and disclose:

- Remuneration policy
- Arrangements for individual directors

Consider allowing members to vote on remuneration statement in accounts.

Service contracts

If service contracts are too long, premature termination may mean significant payments. Service contracts should not be > 12 months.

Risk policy statement

Statement to be distributed to all managers and staff, covering

- Definitions
- Objectives
- Regulations
- Links with strategy
- Key risk management areas
- Key controls
- Roles of staff and managers

Risk register

- Lists and priorities main risks
- Those responsible for dealing with risks
- Actions taken and resulting risk levels

Risk management personnel

- Board
- Risk committee
- Risk managers/specialists
- Operational managers and staff
- Internal and external audit

Risk management function

- Set policy and strategy
- Build risk awareness and competence
- Establish risk management policy
- Design and review of processes
- Implement risk indicators and reports
- Prepare reports on risk

Board review

Boards need to consider:

- Nature and extent of significant risks taken
- Threat of risks materialising
- Ability to reduce risk incidence/impact
- Costs and benefits of controls
- Frequency of monitoring

Monitoring

- Change identification/management
- Communication to right people
- Related to organisational size/complexity
- Formality

Internal risk reporting

Reporting needs to be:

- Comprehensive
- Regular
- Frequent for high impact-likelihood risks

Reporting needs to include:

- Comparisons actual v predicted risk
- Feedback on risk reduction
- Details of residual risk

External risk reporting

- Board responsibility
- Risk management process
- Review of effectiveness
- Impact of problems

USA Sarbanes-Oxley

- Disclose deficiencies in internal control to auditors and audit committee
- Acknowledge responsibilities for internal control in accounts and assess effectiveness based on evaluation 30 days prior to report
- Disclose any material weaknesses in internal controls over financial reporting

UK

- The review of internal control should be an integral part of the company's operations (Turnbull).
- Companies should explain their business model (UK Corporate Governance Code)

Relationships with shareholders

Directors should be held accountable by requiring them to submit to regular re-election (every three years). Boards should consider relationships with all shareholders, particularly institutional shareholders.

Hampel recommendations

- Send notice of AGM at least 20 working days before meeting
- Provide business presentation at AGM
- Question and answers sessions at AGM with committee chairman
- Shareholders vote separately on each substantially separate issue
- Shareholders vote on report and accounts

Relationships with stakeholders

OECD stresses role of:

- Employees
- Creditors
- Suppliers
- Shareholders
- Government

Position of stakeholders should be:

- Part of corporate governance
- Enhanced by participation (eg employees share ownership, profit-sharing arrangements)

3: Ethics and reputation

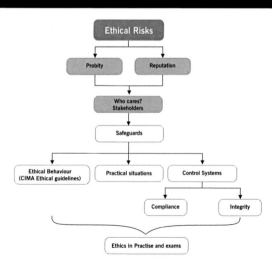

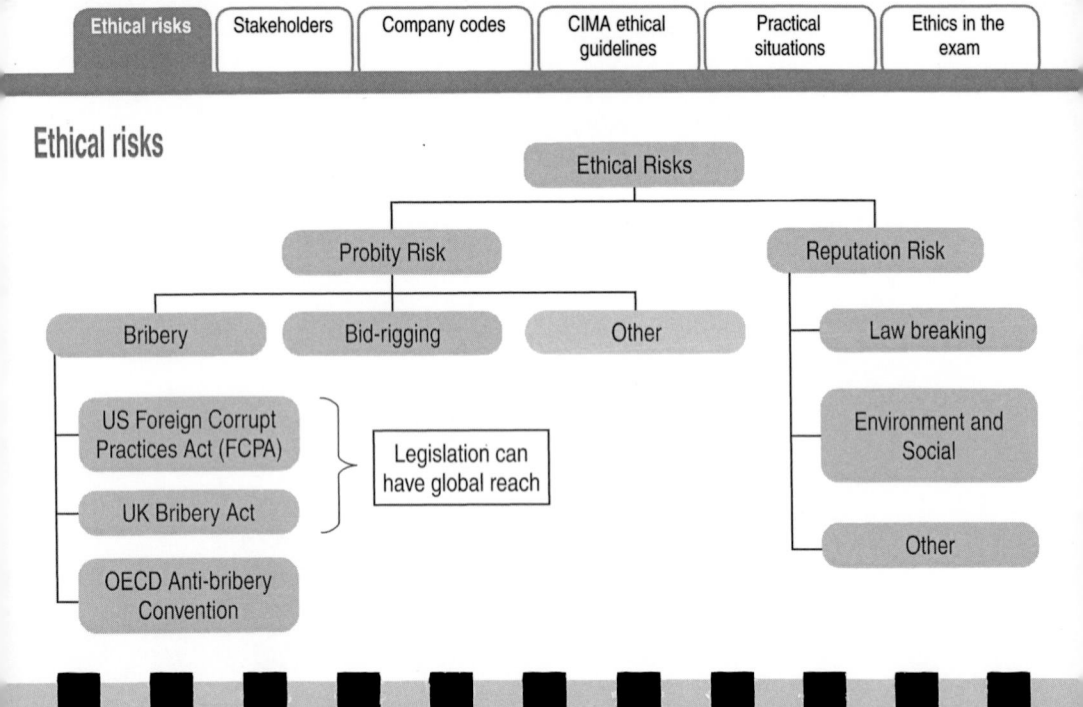

Stakeholder claims

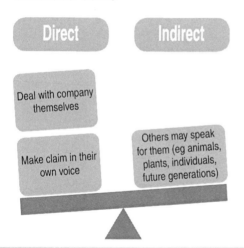

Direct

Indirect

Deal with company themselves

Make claim in their own voice

Others may speak for them (eg animals, plants, individuals, future generations)

Mendelow's Power/Interest matrix

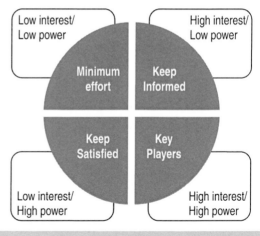

Low interest/ Low power

High interest/ Low power

Minimum effort

Keep Informed

Keep Satisfied

Key Players

Low interest/ High power

High interest/ High power

Code of conduct

Code sets out expectations of ways employees will behave.

However, issuing a code isn't enough, the code needs to be backed by:

- Commitment of senior management
- Staff understanding of importance of ethics
- Staff commitment to ethics

Other measures

- Detailed guidance
- Identity and values stressed
- Training
- Reward schemes
- Whistle-blowing procedures
- Ethical departments/audits

Contents of codes

- Ethical principles
- Commitment required from employees
- Compliance with law
- Treatment of customers
- Treatment of suppliers
- Commitment to fair competition
- Commitment to environment
- Commitment to community
- Corporate citizenship

Problems with codes

Codes may be seen as inflexible and unfair sets of rules, that are not relevant to the ethical situations employees encounter.

Fundamental principles

CIMA's code emphasises the importance of students and members acting in the public interest. The objectives of the accountancy profession require members to produce credible information, show professionalism and deliver good quality services. The public must have confidence in the ethical framework.

Professional behaviour	Protects the reputations of the professional person and the professional body.
Integrity	Accountants must not be party to anything false or misleading.
Professional competence and due care	Perform services with reasonable care, competence and diligence.
Confidentiality	No disclosure of confidential information without permission or legal or professional right or duty.
Objectivity	Avoid all bias, prejudice and partiality.

Ethical conflict

Guard against – often arises where loyalties are divided or pressure is applied.

**T
H
R
E
A
T
S**

Advocacy

Self-interest

Intimidation

Familiarity

Self-review

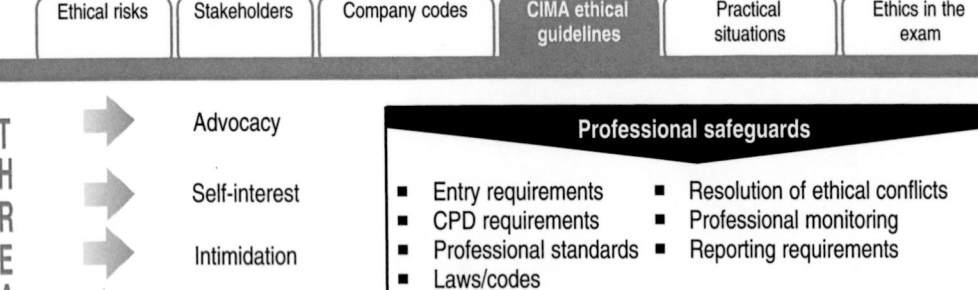

Professional safeguards

- Entry requirements
- CPD requirements
- Professional standards
- Laws/codes
- Resolution of ethical conflicts
- Professional monitoring
- Reporting requirements

Workplace safeguards

- Employer's oversight systems
- Employer's ethics and conduct programmes
- Ethical leadership
- HR/training procedures
- Communication/whistleblowing/consultation

Resolution of ethical conflicts

CIMA suggests:

- Gather all relevant information
- Raise concerns internally
- Raise concerns externally
- Remove self from situation

Professional and employment obligations

Accountants should fulfil legal and ethical obligations, including confidentiality. However accountants may be pressurised to act illegally or unethically, including being responsible for misleading information.

Preparation and reporting of information

Information should describe clearly nature of business transactions, classify and record information in timely and proper manner, and represent facts accurately.

Acting with expertise

Competent performance by accountant may be threatened by lack of time, lack of information, insufficient training, inadequate resources.

Financial interests

Share ownership, share options and profit-related bonuses provide incentives to manipulate information. Disclosure of relevant information counters this threat.

Inducements

Accountants may appear to be compromised by having being offered an inducement as well as accepting one. Accountants need to disclose offer to senior management, also to third parties.

How to gain marks

Marks will be awarded for:

- Analysis of the situation
- Recognition of ethical issues
- Explanations of relevant ethical guidance
- Making clear, logical and appropriate recommendations
- Justifying recommendations in practical business and ethical terms

Step-by-step approach

1. Identify key facts

2. Identify ethical issues and fundamenal principles

3. Consider alternative actions and consequences

4. Recommend action

5. Justify decision

4: IS risks

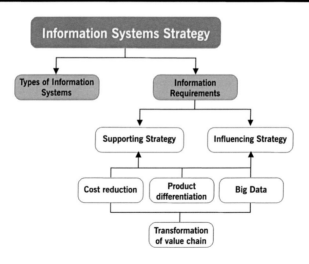

Information requirements

Organisations require information for:

- **Planning:** available resources, possible timescales and likely outcomes

- **Controlling:** assessing whether activities are proceeding as planned and taking corrective action if deviations occur

- **Recording and processing transactions**

- **Performance measurement:** comparisons against budget or plan

- **Decision making:** strategic planning, management control and operational control

Strategic information

Strategic information assists strategic planning, the process of deciding on the objectives of the organisation, and planning how to achieve those objectives.

Characteristics

- Derived from internal and external sources
- Summarised at a high level
- Relevant to the long term
- Deals with whole organisation
- Often prepared on an *ad hoc* basis
- Both quantitative and qualitative

Tactical information

is used to decide how the resources of the business should be employed, and to monitor how they are and have been employed.

Characteristics

- Primarily from internal sources
- Summarised to some extent
- Relevant to the short and medium term
- Deals with activities and/or departments
- Prepared routinely and regularly
- Mainly quantitative

Operational information

is used to ensure that specific operational tasks are planned and carried out as intended. It assists in controlling day-to-day activities of the organisation.

Characteristics

- Derived entirely from internal sources
- Highly detailed
- Relates to immediate/short term
- Task-specific
- Prepared frequently, routinely
- Largely quantitative

Accurate

Complete

Cost-beneficial

User-targeted

Relevant

Authoritative

Timely

Easy to use

'Good' information is information that adds to the understanding of a situation.

Value of information

Information value depends upon:

- Its source
- Ease of assimilation
- Accessibility

Information Systems (IS)

are systems at any level of an organisation that change goals, processes, products, services or environmental relationships with the aim of gaining competitive advantage. Stratigic level IS systems are systems used by senior management for long-term decision making.

Information Technology (IT)

describes the interaction of computer technology and data transmission technology to operate systems that satisfy the organisation's information needs. These include hardware, software and operating systems.

Information Management (IM)

refers to the basic management approach to IS, including planning, environment, control, technology.

Information systems strategy

is the long-term plan concerned with exploiting information systems and technology, either to support business strategies or create new strategic options and competitive advantage.

The IS strategy is supported by the IT strategy and the IM strategy.

Competitive advantage

- Improve productivity and performance
- Alter management and organisational structure of business
- Lead to development of new businesses

Information technology strategy

involves deciding how information needs will be met by balancing supply and demand of funds and facilities, and the development of programmes to supply IT hardware and software.

Information management strategy

aims to ensure that information is provided to users and stored, accessed and controlled and that redundant information is not being produced.

Different types of information systems serve information needs at different levels of an organisation.

Executive Information Systems (EIS) or Executive Support Systems (ESS)

EIS or ESS serve the strategic level of the organisation. They have:

- Menu driven user friendly interfaces
- Interactive graphics to help visualisation of the situation
- Communication capabilities linking the executive to external databases

An ESS summarises and tracks strategically critical information from the MIS and DSS.

Strategic Enterprise Management Systems (SEMS) and Enterprise Resource Planning Systems (ERPS)

SEMS and ERPS operate across organisational systems.

SEMS assist organisations in setting strategic goals, measuring performance, and measuring and managing intellectual capital.

ERPS handle organisational and support functions, and can link with suppliers and customers. They integrate everything into one system. They can support performance measures. ERPS should mean lower costs and investment, increased flexibility and efficiency.

Decision Support Systems (DSS) and Management Information Systems (MIS)

DSS and MIS serve middle management.

The DSS provide information, models, or tools for manipulating and/or analysing information. They support decision-making in semi-structured and unstructured situations eg, portfolio and production planning. An example of a DSS is the spreadsheet.

The MIS are used to keep records, to supply management information and to forecast. They support structured decision-making at operational and management control levels, are relatively inflexible, have an internal focus and are designed to report on existing operations.

Expert Systems

Expert system software uses a knowledge base consisting of facts, concepts and relationships and uses pattern techniques to make judgements and suggest decisions, eg on loan applications. Conditions are:

- Problem is well-defined
- Expert can define rules
- Investment is cost-justified

Expert systems are not suited to higher level, unstructured problems as these require information from a wide range of sources.

Knowledge Work Systems (KWS)

KWS help knowledge workers create and integrate knowledge into the organisation. Examples include CAD.

Office Automation Systems (OAS)

OAS create, handle and manage documents, manage workflow and scheduling, help manage client portfolios and help with communication.

Transaction Processing Systems (TPS)

TPS serve the operational level and support highly structured decisions. They are used for routine tasks where transactions must be processed so that operations can continue eg, sales order entry.

Evaluating information systems

Cost-benefit analysis

All costs and benefits must be compared, including costs of not acting. Difficult to quantify improvements in information.

Other evaluation methods

- Balanced scorecard including impact on management/structure
- Effect on competitive position
- Business case (financial/marketing/operational)
- User requirements

Technical viability

- Available technology
- Available skills
- Risk issues
- Compatibility with existing systems
- User numbers/data amounts

Operational viability

- Data availability/reliability/clarity
- Operational procedures
- Level of support/commitment
- Human resource issues
- Stakeholder impacts

Strategy for IS/IT

A strategy for IS/IT is justified on the grounds that it:

- Involves high costs
- Is critical to the success of many organisations
- Can be used as a source of competitive advantage
- Impacts on customer service
- Affects all levels of management
- Affects the way management information is created and presented
- Requires effective management to obtain maximum benefit
- Involves many stakeholders

Benefits of technological change

- Cuts production costs
- Develops better quality products and services
- Develops new products and services
- Provides products and services more quickly
- Frees staff from repetitive work
- Identifies markets
- Develops new distribution channels
- Removes unnecessary management
- Enhances communications with customers
- Improves management knowledge
- Enhances enterprise co-ordination

Information strategy and The Value Chain

Support activities	Firm infrastructure	Enterprise Resource Planning Intranets Extranets				
	Human resource management	Automated personnel scheduling				
	Technology development	Computer aided design Electronic market research				
	Procurement	Online procurement of parts (e-procurement)				
		Automated warehouse

Electronic data interchange (EDI) | Flexible manufacturing | Automated order processing

Vehicle tracking | Electronic marketing

CRM

EPOS

Remote terminals for salespersons | Remote servicing of equipment

Computer scheduling and routing of repair trucks |
| | | Inbound logistics

Primary activities | Operations | Outbound logistics | Marketing and Service sales | |

Margin

Big Data

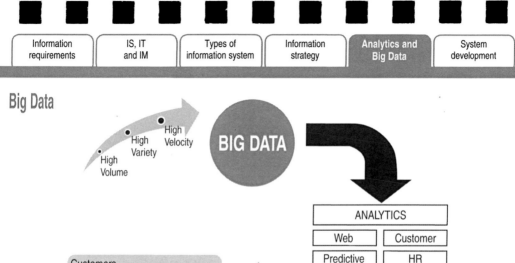

Systems development life cycle

Feasibility study
Briefly review the existing system
Identify possible alternative solutions

Systems investigation
Obtain details of current requirements and user needs such as data volumes, processing cycles and timescales
Identify current problems and restrictions

Systems analysis
Consider why current methods are used and identify better alternatives

Systems design
Determine what inputs, processing and storage facilities are necessary to produce the outputs required
Consider matters such as program design, file design and security
Prepare a detailed specification of the new system
Test it

Systems implementation
Write or acquire software, test it, convert files, install hardware and start running the new system

Review and maintenance
Ensure that the new system meets current objectives, and that it continues to do so

Testing

Testing should involve:

- Systems logic
- Programs
- Overall system
- Useability and user acceptance

Staffing and training

Training will be needed when a new system is introduced, an existing system changed or new staff are recruited.

Steering committee oversees development.
Project team, including IT specialists and users, is responsible for detailed planning, design, development and implementation.

File conversion

Conversion of existing files into format suitable for new system. Possible methods:

- Direct changeover
- Parallel running
- Pilot operation
- Phased changeover

Post-implementation review

A post-implementation review should establish whether system objectives and performance criteria have been met, and if not, why not – and what should be done about it.

Notes

5: Financial risk

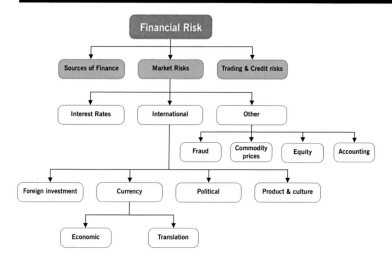

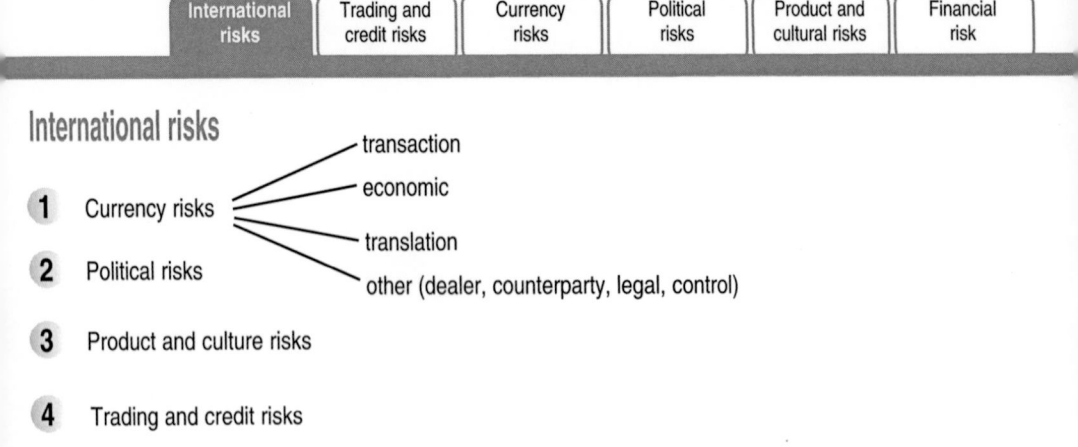

International risks | Trading and credit risks | Currency risks | Political risks | Product and cultural risks | Financial risk

International risks

1. Currency risks
   - transaction
   - economic
   - translation
   - other (dealer, counterparty, legal, control)

2. Political risks

3. Product and culture risks

4. Trading and credit risks

Control of international risks

A business can reduce its exposure to international risks by diversification of its trading interests or portfolio of investments.

Foreign trade

Foreign trade has various features that may mean payment is delayed, including extended credit, time needed to arrange exports, paperwork and transport time.

Physical risk	The risk of goods or documentation being lost or stolen in-transit
Credit risk	Possibility of payment default by customer
Trade risk	The risk of the customer refusing to accept the goods or the cancellation of the order
Liquidity risk	Inability to finance the credit

Controlling credit risk

- Export factoring
- Forfaiting
- Documentary credits
- International credit unions
- Export credit insurance
- Acceptance credits
- Export merchants
- Government departments

Economic exposure

is the risk that exchange rate movements might reduce the international competitiveness of a company.

Controlling economic exposure

- Matching assets and liabilities
- Diversifying supplier and customer base
- Diversifying operations worldwide

Translation exposure

is the risk that the organisation will make exchange losses when the accounting results and position of its foreign branches or subsidiaries are translated into home currency.

Translation exposure probably does not need to be hedged. Sometimes it may be hedged if a business believes that investors will be unhappy with translation losses.

Political risks

Political risks can arise through various forms of government actions, such as:

- Quotas, limiting quantities
- Tariffs, making imports more expensive
- Legal standards
- Restrictions on foreign ownership
- Nationalisation

Controlling political risks

- Negotiate concessions
- Insurance
- Production strategies
- Maintain contact with markets
- Financial management
- Threaten withdrawal

Blocked funds

Blocked funds arise from restrictions on types of transaction for which payments abroad allowed, such as bans on dividends to overseas shareholders.

Controlling blocked funds

- Sales of goods and services to subsidiary
- Royalty charges
- Interest on loans
- Management charges

Legal risks

The risks of problems with legal systems including:

- Suffering penalties due to non-compliance with laws
- Expending resources to ensure compliance
- Suffering losses through inability to enforce legal rights (such as copyright)

Dealing with legal risks

- Legal action (costly)
- Relocation of operations to where legal burden is lower
- Ensure awareness of relevant regulations
- Lobby for/to prevent changes
- Act as good citizen, complying with voluntary codes

Cultural risks

Cultural risks are the risks of suffering disruption through problems with overseas staff, or the risk of losing business overseas through failing to understand local practices and ways of doing business.

Dealing with cultural risks

- Enter markets where culture is compatible
- Adapt products to local conditions
- Use appropriate control systems (centralisation/decentralisation balance)
- Use of expatriate staff (consider cost, failure of expatriates to adjust to local culture)
- Give local staff opportunities/appropriate training

Sensitivity analysis

Sensitivity analysis is a modelling and risk assessment process in which changes are made to significant variables in order to determine the effect of these changes on the outcome. Particular attention is then paid to variables identified as being of special significance.

Key variables

- Selling price
- Sales volume
- Cost of capital
- Initial cost
- Operating costs
- Benefits

Example

NPV of a project with an initial investment of £500,000 is £80,000. The initial investment can rise by (80,000/500,000) × 100% =16% before the investment just breaks even.

Weaknesses

- Difficult to analyse interdependencies
- Change in more than one variable can't be calculated this way
- No indication of likelihood
- May be difficult to control critical factors
- Managers decide what is acceptable

Certainty equivalent approach

The certainty equivalent approach involves converting expected cash flows into equivalent risk-free amounts and discounting at the risk-free rate. The greater the risk of the expected cash flow:

- The smaller the certainty equivalent receipt
- The larger the certainty equivalent payment

Disadvantages of certainty equivalents

- Adjustments to cash flows decided subjectively
- Ascertaining the risk-free rate

Expected values (EV)

The EV of an opportunity is equal to the sum of (the probability of an outcome occurring (p) × return expected if it does occur (x)) = Σpx.

The calculation of EVs is more useful when outcomes occur many times over.

Expected values and NPV

1. Calculate NPV

2. Measure risk:
   - Worst outcome and probability
   - Probability negative result
   - Standard deviation of NPV

Regression analysis

Measures sensitivity of cash flows to various risk factors.

Simulations

Used to assess projects with lots of outcomes, or projects with correlated cash flows.

Scenarios

Used as a means of predicting alternative situations based on changing conditions. They can be used to quantify possible losses and as a basis for developing **contingency plans**.

Value at risk (VAR)

Mean – (confidence interval value for $X\%$ × standard deviation)

Example

Possible gains or losses on daily trading normally distributed around mean of 0 + daily standard deviation of £10,000. Daily VAR at 5% confidence is

1 Daily volatility – £10,000

2 Normal value 95(100 − 5)% = 1.65

3 VAR = 1.65 × 10,000 = £16,500

5% chance daily loss > £16,500

| International risks | Trading and credit risks | Currency risks | Political risks | Product and cultural risks | Financial risk |

Hedging

Hedging means designating one or more hedging instruments so that change in fair value is offset by change in fair value or cash flows of hedged items.

- **Fair value** hedges – recognise in profit or loss
- **Cash flow** hedges – recognise effective portion in other comprehensive income
- Disclose hedges + risks being hedged

Organisational aims

- Value assets, liabilities, derivatives
- Produce documentation of hedging strategies
- Provide testing of effectiveness
- Managing hedging relationships
- Generate necessary information
- Accomodate IAS requirements

Notes

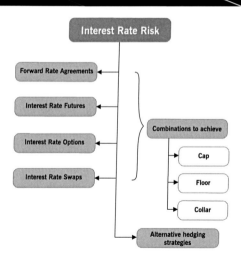

Sources of risk

1 Fixed v floating rate debt

2 Currency of debt

3 Term of loan

4 Term loan v overdraft

Interest rate risk management

- Netting
- Smoothing
- Matching
- Pooling
- Forward rate agreements
- Interest rate futures
- Interest rate options or guarantees
- Interest rate swaps

Interest rate risk is often not hedged because of the costs, lack of availability of appropriate instruments, remoteness of risk crystallising or immateriality of impact if the risk does crystallise.

Forward rate agreement (FRA)

is an agreement, typically between a company and a bank, to fix the interest rate charged/received on future borrowing or bank deposits.

A 3-9 FRA starts in three months and lasts for six months.

FRAs	
Advantages	*Disadvantages*
■ Protection provided	■ Rate > current market
■ Flexibility on time and size	■ Falling interest rate
	■ FRAs expire and need to be renegotiated
■ Low cost	■ No market for these

Netting

Aggregating and hedging net exposure.

Smoothing

Maintaining a balance between fixed and floating rate borrowing.

Matching

Matching assets and liabilities that have a common interest rate.

Pooling

If organisation has different accounts with same bank, pooling balances for interest charges and overdraft limits.

Interest rate futures

Interest rate futures hedge against interest rate movements. The terms, amounts and periods are standardised:

- The futures prices will vary with changes in interest rates
- Outlay to buy futures is less than buying the financial instrument
- Price of short-term futures quoted at discount to 100 Par value (93.40 indicates deposit trading at 6.6%)

Interest rate futures	
Advantages	*Disadvantages*
■ Cost	■ Inflexibility of terms
■ Amount hedged	■ Basis risk
■ Traded so can be sold on	■ Daily settlement

| Interest rate risk | FRAs and pooling | Interest rate futures | Interest rate options | Interest rate swaps |

Interest rate option

grants the buyer the right, but not the obligation, to deal at an agreed interest rate at a future maturity date.

If a company wishes to hedge **borrowing, purchase put options**.

If a company wishes to hedge **lending, purchase call options**.

Strike price	Puts			Calls		
	Nov	Dec	Jan	Nov	Dec	Jan
113.50	0.87	1.27	1.34	0.29	0.69	1.06

- Strike price is price paid for futures contract
- Numbers under each month represent premium paid for option contract
- Put options more expensive than call as interest rates predicted to rise

Valuation of options

Black-Scholes model measures impact of factors affecting value:

- Current value
- Exercise price
- Time to expiry
- Variability of share price
- Risk-free rate of return

Interest rate cap sets an interest rate ceiling.   **Interest rate floor** sets lower limit to interest rates.

Interest rate collar means can buy interest rate cap and sell floor. Zero-cost collar is when premium for buying cap equals premium for selling floor.

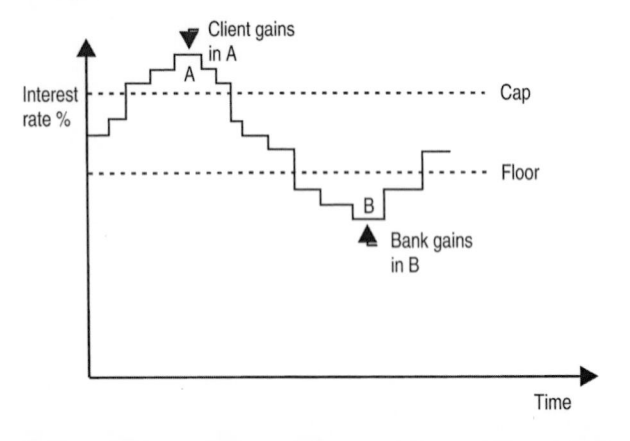

Interest rate swaps

are transactions that exploit different interest rates in different markets for borrowing, to reduce interest costs for either fixed or floating rate loans.

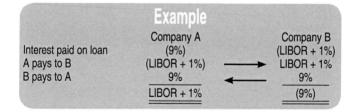

Example

	Company A	Company B
Interest paid on loan	(9%)	(LIBOR + 1%)
A pays to B	(LIBOR + 1%)	LIBOR + 1%
B pays to A	9%	9%
	LIBOR + 1%	(9%)

6: Financial risk – Interest rate risk

Advantages

- Flexibility and costs
- Use of credit ratings
- Capital restructuring
- Risk management
- Easy to arrange
- Predictability of cash flows

Disadvantages

- Counterparty risk
- Become subject to floating interest rates
- Lack of liquid market
- Costs/time not worth benefits

Uses of interest rate swaps

- Switching from paying one type of interest to another
- Raising less expensive loans
- Securing better deposit rates
- Managing interest rate risk
- Avoiding charges for loan termination

7: International risk – Exchange rates

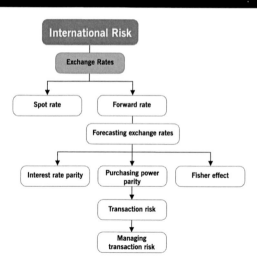

Direct quote is amount of domestic currency equal to one foreign currency unit.

Indirect quote is amount of foreign currency equal to one domestic unit.

Remember!

Company sells base currency LOW
buys base currency HIGH

For example, if UK company is buying and selling pounds, selling (offer) price may be 1.45 $ per £, buying (bid) price may be 1.47 $ per £.

Influences on exchange rates

- Interest rates
- Inflation rates
- Balance of payments
- Market sentiment/speculation
- Government policy

Remember!

If the exchange rate is Home 1 unit = Foreign X units DIVIDE foreign currency amount by rate.

If the exchange rate is Foreign 1 unit = Home X units MULTIPLY foreign currency amount by rate.

Interest rate parity	Future spot rate A/B = Spot rate A/B $\times \dfrac{1 + \text{B's interest rate}}{1 + \text{A's interest rate}}$
Purchasing power parity	Future spot rate A/B = Spot rate A/B $\times \dfrac{1 + \text{B's inflation rate}}{1 + \text{A's inflation rate}}$

Transaction risk

is the risk of adverse exchange rate movements between the date the price is agreed and cash is received/paid, arising during normal international trade.

Netting

The process of setting off credit against debit balances so that only the net amounts are paid by currency flows. **Multilateral netting** involves offsetting several companies' balances.

Invoicing in buyer's currency

This means that the exporter bears exchange risk but may have marketing advantages/market may require invoicing in particular currency (US dollar). Exporter may be able to offset payments in foreign currency, and may be able to obtain loan on favourable terms.

Other direct risk reduction methods

- Invoicing in own currency
- Matching receipts and payments
- Lead payments (payments in advance)
- Lagged payments (delaying payments)
- Matching assets and liabilities
- Countertrade

Forward exchange contract

A firm and binding contract

For the purchase/sale of a specified quantity of a stated foreign currency

At a rate fixed at the time the contract is made

For performance at a future time agreed when contract is made

Forward rate

An exchange rate set for currencies to be exchanged at a future date.

Forward rates as adjustments to spot rates

| Forward rate cheaper | – | Quoted at discount |
| Forward rate more expensive | – | Quoted at premium |

Advantages

☑ Any amount

☑ Flexible length

Disadvantages

☒ Counterparty default

☒ Difficult to cancel

Money market hedging

Future foreign currency payment	Future foreign currency receipt
1 Borrow now in home currency	1 Borrow now in foreign currency
2 Convert home currency loan to foreign currency	2 Convert foreign currency loan to home currency
3 Put foreign currency on deposit	3 Put home currency on deposit
4 When have to make payment	4 When cash received
(a) Make payment from deposit	(a) Take cash from deposit
(b) Repay home currency borrowing	(b) Repay foreign currency borrowing

8: International risk – Financial instruments

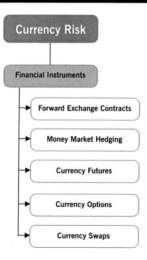

Futures terminology

Futures contract	Obliges buyer/seller to purchase/sell specified quantity at predetermined price when contract expires
Contract size	Fixed minimum quantity of currency bought or sold using futures contract
Basis	Spot price – futures price
Basis risk	The risk that futures price movement may differ from underlying movement
Settlement date	The date when trading on a futures contract ceases and accounts are settled
Tick size	Smallest measured unit in contract price

| Futures terminology | Currency futures | Currency options | Currency swaps |

What type of contract

Transaction on future date		Now		On future date	
Receive	currency	Sell	currency futures	Buy	currency futures
Pay	currency	Buy	currency futures	Sell	currency futures
Receive	$	Buy	currency futures	Sell	currency futures
Pay	$	Sell	currency futures	Buy	current futures

Advantages and disadvantages of futures contracts

Advantages

- Transaction costs lower than forward contracts
- Exact date of receipt or payment doesn't have to be known
- Low counterparty risk on traded markets

Disadvantages

- Can't tailor to user's exact needs
- Only available in limited number of currencies
- Hedge inefficiencies

Step 1 Setup

(a) Choose which contract (settlement date after date currency needed)

(b) Choose type of contract (buy or sell)

(c) Choose number of contracts $\dfrac{\text{Amount being hedged}}{\text{Size of contract}}$

Convert using today's futures contract price if amount being hedged is in US dollars

Step 2 Estimate closing futures price

You should be given this

Step 3 Hedge outcome

(a) **Outcome in futures market**

Opening futures price

Closing futures price

Futures profit   Movement in rate × Value of one contract × Number of contracts

(b) **Net outcome**

Spot market payment (at closing spot rate)	(X)
Futures profit/(loss) (at closing spot rate unless US company)	X
Net outcome	(X)

Currency option

A right to buy or sell currency at a stated rate of exchange at some time in the future.

Call – right to buy at fixed rate

Put – right to sell at fixed rate

Over the counter options — Tailor-made options suited to a company's specific needs.

Traded options — Contracts for standardised currency amounts, only available in certain currencies.

Choosing the right option

Complicated by lack of US dollar traded options. UK company wishing to sell US dollars can purchase £ call options (options to buy sterling with dollars).

Why option is needed

- Uncertainty about foreign currency receipts or payments (timing and amount)
- Support tender for overseas contract
- Allow publication of price lists in foreign currency
- Protect import/export of price-sensitive goods

What type of option

Transaction on future date			Now		On future date	
Receive	currency	Buy	currency put	Sell	currency
Pay	currency	Buy	currency call	Buy	currency
Receive	$	Buy	currency call	Buy	currency
Pay	$	Buy	currency put	Sell	currency

Drawbacks of options	Option premiums
■ Cost dependent on expected volatility ■ Pay on purchase ■ Tailor-made options aren't negotiable ■ Traded options not in every currency	■ The exercise price ■ Maturity date ■ Volatility and interest rates ■ Interest rate differentials

Step 1 Set up the hedge

(a) Choose contract date

(b) Decide whether put or call option required

(c) Decide which strike price applies and hence which premium

(d) Decide how many contracts, converting if necessary

(e) Calculate premium using spot rate

Step 2 Ascertain closing prices

You should be given it/them.

Step 3 Calculate outcome of hedge

(a) **Outcome in options market**

Exercise?

(b) **Net outcome**

	Yes £	No £
Spot market payment (closing spot rate)	—	(X)
Option market outcome (translate balance at closing spot rate unless US company)	(X)	—
Option premium (opening spot rate unless US company)	(X)	(X)
Net outcome	(X)	(X)

Currency swaps

In a currency swap, equivalent amounts of currency are swapped for a period. However the original borrower remains liable to the lender (counterparty risk).

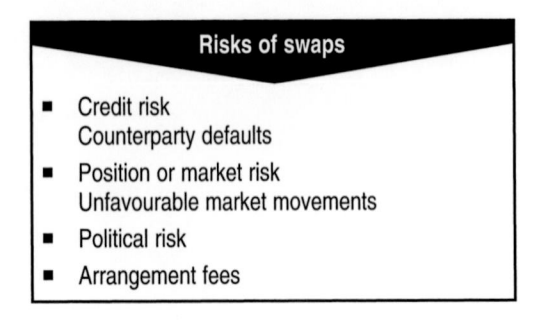

Risks of swaps

- Credit risk
  Counterparty defaults
- Position or market risk
  Unfavourable market movements
- Political risk
- Arrangement fees

Advantages of currency swaps

- Flexibility – any size and reversible
- Low transaction costs
- Not exposed to foreign exchange markets
- Can gain access to debt in other countries
- Restructuring currency base of liabilities
- Conversion of fixed to/from floating rate debt
- Absorb excess liquidity

Example

Edward Ltd wishes to borrow US dollars to finance an investment in America. Edward's treasurer is concerned about the high interest rates the company faces because it is not well-known in America. Edward Ltd could make an arrangement with an American company, Gordon Inc, attempting to borrow sterling in the UK money markets.

Step 1

Gordon borrows US $ and Edward borrows £. The two companies then swap funds at the current spot rate.

Step 2

Edward pays the £ interest and receives the £ interest from Gordon. Gordon pays the $ interest and receives the $ interest from Edward.

Step 3

At the end of the period the two companies swap back the principal amounts at the spot rate/predetermined rate.

9: Investment risk

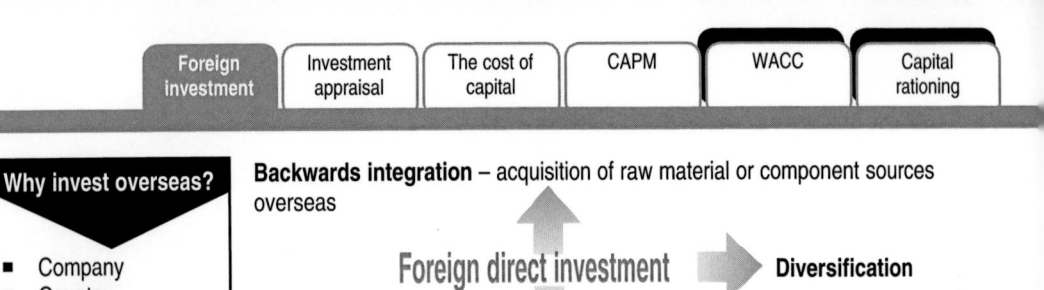

Why invest overseas?

- Company
- Country
- Customer
- Competition
- Currency

Backwards integration – acquisition of raw material or component sources overseas

Foreign direct investment → **Diversification**

Forward integration – establishing final production and distribution outlets overseas

Means

- New start-up investments
- Overseas takeover/merger means of acquiring market share and distribution channels
- Joint ventures
  - contractual
  - joint equity

Alternatives

- Exporting directly, or through agents
- Licensing, giving overseas producers rights to production process in return for royalties
- **Countertrade** – non arms-length transaction, including barter, counterpurchase and offset

Purpose of setting up subsidiaries	Risks of overseas investments
<ul><li>Location of markets</li><li>Sales organisation</li><li>Opportunity to produce goods more cheaply</li><li>Avoid import controls</li><li>Obtain access to raw materials</li><li>Availability of grants and tax concessions</li></ul>	<ul><li>Foreign exchange risk<ul><li>Higher costs or lower revenues</li><li>Accounting losses on translation</li></ul></li><li>Political risk</li><li>Geographical separation leading to control problems</li><li>Litigation risks</li><li>Risk of loss of goods in transit</li></ul>

Consider use of overseas debt finance, transfer pricing, matching overseas assets and liabilities, joint ventures.

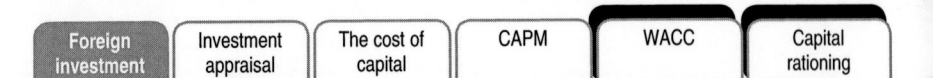

Internal hedging techniques

- Invoicing in home currency
- Matching
- Leading and lagging
- Netting

External hedging techniques

- Forward contracts
- Money market hedge
- Futures
- Options

Double taxation relief

is an agreement between two countries intended to avoid double taxation of income.

Forecasting exchange rates

can be done using purchasing power parity/interest rate parity.

Two techniques for foreign investment appraisal

1 Convert the project cash flows into sterling and discount at a sterling discount rate.

2 Discount the cash flows in the foreign currency at an adjusted discount rate for that currency and convert resulting NPV at spot exchange rate.

Example

Current spot rate is \$/£0.667, (that is, \$1 = £0.667)
UK inflation 3%, US inflation 1%

$$\text{Forward rate } \$/£ = \text{Spot } \$/£ \times \frac{1 + \text{UK inflation rate}}{1 + \text{US inflation rate}}$$

$$= 0.667 \times \frac{1 + 0.03}{1 + 0.01}$$

$$= 0.680$$

International investment appraisal

Foreign currency cash flows	Time					
	0	1	2	3	4	5
Sales receipts		X	X	X	X	
Costs		(X)	(X)	(X)	(X)	
Tax allowable depreciation		(X)	(X)	(X)	(X)	
Taxable profit		X	X	X	X	
Taxation			(X)	(X)	(X)	(X)
Tax allowable depreciation		X	X	X	X	
Capital expenditure	(X)					
Scrap value					X	
Tax on scrap value						(X)
Terminal value					X	
Tax on terminal value						(X)
Working capital	(X)	(X)	(X)	X	X	
	(X)	X	X	X	X	(X)

	Time					
	0	1	2	3	4	5
Exchange rates	X	X	X	X	X	X
Domestic cash flows						
Invested in/remitted						
from foreign country	(X)	X	X	X	X	(X)
Additional domestic tax			(X)	(X)	(X)	(X)
Additional domestic expenses/income		(X)	(X)	(X)	(X)	
Domestic tax effect of domestic						
expenses/income	—	—	X	X	X	X
Net domestic cash flows	(X)	X	X	X	X	(X)
Discount factors @ domestic%	X	X	X	X	X	X
Present values	(X)	X	X	X	X	(X)

The cost of capital

is the rate of return that the enterprise must pay to satisfy the providers of funds and it reflects the riskiness of providing funds.

Risk free rate of return —————————■ Return required from a completely risk free investment eg yield on government securities

+

Premium for business risk —————————■ Increase in required rate of return due to uncertainty about future and business prospects

+

Premium for financial risk —————————■ Danger of high debt levels, variability of equity returns

COST OF CAPITAL

The capital asset pricing model (CAPM)

can be used to calculate the cost of equity and incorporate **risk**.

Beta factor (β)

measures the systematic risk of a security relative to the market. It is the average fall in the return on a share each time there is a 1% fall in the stock market as a whole.

Unsystematic risk

- Specific to the company
- Can be reduced or eliminated by diversification

Systematic risk

- Due to variations in market activity
- Cannot be diversified away

Increasing risk

→

Beta < 1.0
Share < average risk
K_e < average

Beta = 1.0
Share = average risk
K_e = average

Beta > 1.0
Share > average risk
K_e > average

9: Investment risk

The CAPM formula

$$k_e = R_f + (R_m - R_f)\,\beta$$

where $k_e(r_i)$ is cost of equity capital/expected equity return

      R_f is risk-free rate of return

      R_m is return from market

      β is beta factor of security

Market risk premium

is the extra return required from a share to compensate for its risk compared with average market risk.

Problems with CAPM

Assumptions unrealistic?

- Zero insolvency costs
- Investment market efficient
- Investors hold well-diversified portfolios'
- Perfect capital market

Required estimates difficult to make

- Excess return
- Risk-free rate (govt. securities' rates vary with lending terms)
- β factors difficult to calculate

Assumptions of WACC

- Project small relative to company and has same business risk as company
- WACC reflects company's long-term future capital structure and costs
- New investments financed by new funds
- Cost of capital reflects marginal cost

Problems with WACC

- New investments may have different business risk
- New finance may change capital structure and perceived financial risk
- Cost of floating rate capital not easy to calculate

Capital rationing

is where an entity has a limited amount of money to invest and investments have to be compared in order to allocate money most effectively.

Soft capital rationing
Internal factors

- Reluctance to cede control
- Wish to use only retained earnings
- Reluctance to dilute EPS
- Reluctance to pay more interest
- Capital expenditure budgets

Relaxation of capital constraints

- Joint ventures
- Licensing/franchising
- Contracting out
- Other sources of finance

Hard capital rationing
External factors

- Depressed stock market
- Restrictions on bank lending
- Conservative lending policies
- Issue costs

Profitability index

$$PI = \frac{\text{NPV of project}}{\text{Initial cash outflow}} \longrightarrow \text{The NPV per \$ invested}$$

Assumptions of PI method

- Opportunity to undertake project lost if not taken during capital rationing period
- Compare uncertainty about project outcomes
- Projects are divisible
- Ignore strategic value
- Ignore cash flow patterns
- Ignore project sizes

Single period rationing with indivisible projects

- If projects are not divisible, PI method may not give optimal solution
- Unused capital

Use trial and error and test NPV available from different combinations of projects.

Option to follow-on (call option)

Investing in a project may lead to other possibilities or options which are valuable, but have not been included in the NPV calculation.

↓

Valuation of real options

- Initial costs and benefits
- Present value of future costs and benefits
- Variability of future costs and benefits
- Timescale to make decision
- Cost of capital

Option to abandon (put option)

Easy to sell assets if project fails or redeploy assets for another use. Could be valuable if future benefit streams are uncertain.

Option to wait (call option)

Generally there is a time period over which a project can be postponed (corresponding to option exercise period). New information may emerge that will aid decision-making.

Adjusted present value (APV)

incorporates the **effects of financing** on the present value of a project.

Step 1.

Evaluate project as if all equity financed by ungearing beta or WACC and calculating NPV using the ungeared k_e. (base case NPV)

$$k_{eg} = k_{eu} + [k_{eu} - k_d] \frac{V_D (1-t)}{V_E} \quad \text{Exam formula}$$

Step 2.

Make adjustments to base case NPV to allow for effects of financing method used.

Advantages of APV method

- Can be used to evaluate **all** the effects of financing
- You do not have to adjust the WACC using assumptions of perpetual risk-free debt

Difficulties with APV method

- Establishing suitable cost of equity
- Identifying all financing costs
- Choosing correct discount rates

Complications in APV calculations

- Issue costs – be careful with calculations and need to discount tax effect
- Increased debt capacity – Incremental effect is tax shield of increased debt finance
- Subsidised borrowing – Include savings in interest and tax shield effect discounted at normal cost of borrowing

10: Internal controls

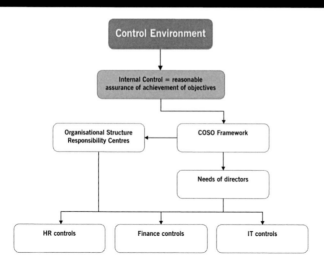

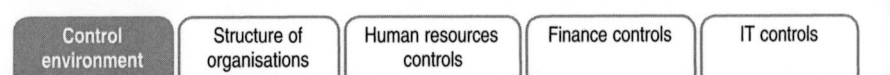
Control environment

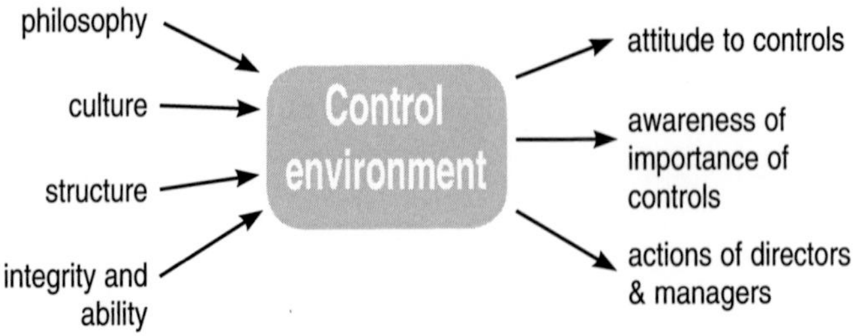

```
philosophy ─────┐
                 ↓
culture ──────→ ┌──────────────┐ ──→ attitude to controls
                │   Control    │
structure ────→ │ environment  │ ──→ awareness of
                │              │      importance of
integrity and ─→└──────────────┘      controls
  ability                       ──→ actions of directors
                                     & managers
```

Turnbull Report

- Strategy for risk
- Culture, codes, policies
- Competence and integrity
- Defined authority, responsibility & accountability
- Communication

COSO framework

Components of organisation

Strategic apex	Directors
Operating core	People involved in process of adding value
Middle line	Middle managers, link between strategic centre and operating core
Techno structure	Finance dept, HRM, designers of controls
Support staff	Marketing, IT, legal, financial

Tall and flat organisations

Tall organisations have a lot of management layers, too rigid and block initiative.

Flat organisations have relatively few levels, allow delegation and empowerment.

Empowerment

- Work teams achieve / set targets
- Delayering of command chain
- Flexibility to serve customer needs
- Encourages knowledge workers + new IT

Hierarchies

Organisation's hierarchy embodies relationships of responsibility, direction and control.

Influences on structure

- Age (greater formality if older)
- Size (if big, more elaborate structure, bigger units, greater formality)
- Information technology
- Dynamism of environment (more fluid if high)
- Complexity of environment (decentralisation)
- External hostility/control (centralisation)
- Power needs (centralisation)

Centralisation and decentralisation

Degree to which authority is delegated.

Centralisation

- Decisions centrally co-ordinated
- Easier for central managers to devise strategy and keep balance
- Better quality strategic decision making
- Enables standardisation

Decentralisation

- Avoids overburdening central management
- Improved local motivation
- Greater awareness of local problems
- Better quality operational/tactical decision making
- Enables local managers to develop

Functional organisation

Departments defined by functions (the work they do).

Advantages

- ☑ Logical
- ☑ Economies of scale

Disadvantages

- ☒ Doesn't reflect value creation
- ☒ Lack of whole business view
- ☒ Lack of co-ordination

Matrix organisation

Dual command structure, perhaps management by product as well as by function. Subordinates have two or more superiors.

Advantages

- ☑ Flexibility
- ☑ Improved communication/co-operation
- ☑ Multiple orientation

Disadvantages

- ☒ Conflicts between managers
- ☒ Greater stress for individuals
- ☒ Complex

Divisionalisation

Divisions are strategic business units with local autonomy. They can be constructed on the basis of geography, product, customers or technology.

Outsourcing

Outsourcing is use of external suppliers to supply products or services.

- Frees up internal time and resources
- Makes specialist expertise available
- Cost – effectiveness
- Needs monitoring of quality of services
- Staff unhappiness/loss of skills
- Transfer of sensitive data

Business process re-engineering

A reorganisation of the organisation's activities in response to the demands of the business environment.

- Radical changes to ways of doing business
- Changing structures in response to customer requirements
- Address lack of staff accountability

Horizontal organisation

Organisation structure based on cross-functional process:

- Team-focused
- Process ownership
- Customer drives process

Human resource management (HRM)

Coherent and strategic approach to managing the organisation's most valuable assets, the people working there.

Control techniques include recruitment and selection, contracts of employment, role definition, training and appraisals.

Behaviour control

- How work performed
- Sequence of tasks
- Used when difficult to assess outcomes
- Legal requirements
- Risk avoidance

Management performance measures

- Subjective ranking, measures
- Outsider judgements
- Upward appraisal
- Tailored accounting measures
- Non-financial measures such as market share

Output control

- Sales/profitability level
- Service delivery
- Operational standards
- Performance targets

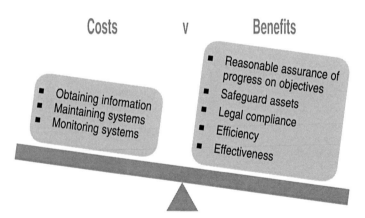

Costs   v   Benefits

Costs
- Obtaining information
- Maintaining systems
- Monitoring systems

Benefits
- Reasonable assurance of progress on objectives
- Safeguard assets
- Legal compliance
- Efficiency
- Effectiveness

Risks

- Income not received
- Assets taken
- Assets deteriorate
- No authorisation
- Poor stakeholder relationships
- Incorrect recording of transactions

Controls

- Segregation of duties
- Documentation
- Reconciliations
- Physical security checks
- Authorisation processes
- Confirm information with stakeholders

Physical access controls

Physical access controls are designed to prevent intruders accessing computer equipment:

- Personnel – receptionists and security guards
- Door locks
- Keypad access system/card entry
- Intruder alarms
- Personnel identification systems

Application controls

The main controls over computer applications are:

- Input – data verification and validation
- Processing – accuracy and completeness
- Output – error reports and distribution
- Back-up – regular copies and storage off-site

Passwords

are a set of characters which may be allocated to a person, a terminal or a facility, which are required to be keyed into the system before further access is permitted to prevent unauthorised access/entry.

They enable:

- Identification of user
- Authentication of user identity
- Checks on user authority
- Restrictions of tasks/access to parts of system

Problems with passwords

- Some can be guessed easily
- Standard passwords not removed
- Users tell unauthorised persons
- Passwords left lying around

Notes

11: Control failures

Risks to operations

Physical damage

- Natural threats (fire, water, storms)
- Human threats (malicious, accidental)

Systems

- Human error
- Technical error
- Data transfer
- Fraud
- Commercial espionage
- Malicious damage
- Industrial action

Internet risks

- Viruses
- Deliberate damage by employees
- Hackers
- Denial of service attacks

Other risks

- Data protection risks
- Project delivery failure
- Audit failure
- Compliance with rules, legal requirements

Security management

Security means protection from unauthorised access, modification, theft or destruction.

Control frameworks

- Benchmarks
- Critical success factors
- Key performance indicators

Security policy

Systematic approach to risk management covering most significant risks, control measures and contingency plans.

Management responsibilities

Top management	Establish strategy, operational responsibilities and contingency plan
Risk manager	Establish procedures, risk assessment, controls, training
Operational manager	Ensure operations meet security requirements
Human resources	Establish recruitment, appraisal, job rotation and division of duties

11: Control failures

Controls over physical threats

Fire
- Site preparation eg fire proof materials
- Detection eg smoke detectors
- Extinguishers eg sprinklers
- Staff training

Water
- Waterproof ceilings and floors
- Adequate drainage

Other measures
- Physical access controls
- Good office layout
- Protected power supplies
- Separate generator
- Regular maintenance programmes

Contingency planning

A **contingency** is an unscheduled interruption of operations that requires measures outside the day-to-day routine operating procedures.

A **contingency plan** (or **disaster recovery plan**) is a plan, formulated in advance, to be implemented upon the occurrence of certain specific future events.

Contingency plan contents

- Definition of responsibilities
- Priorities
- Backup and standby arrangements
- Communication with staff
- Public relations
- Risk assessment

Theft

Small and portable equipment can easily be stolen.

Controls to mitigate theft of equipment

- Maintain equipment log
- Lock equipment away
- Site security measures

IT fraud

Software piracy is the unlicensed use of software by staff on an organisation's machines, or staff illegally copying software owned by the organisation.

Software piracy controls

- Buying from reputable dealers
- Maintaining purchasing and licensing records
- Maintaining central disk store
- Spot inventory checks

Fraud

Computer fraud usually involves theft of funds by dishonest use of computer.

Fraud prevention controls

- Involvement of internal audit
- Computer skills in internal audit
- Computer security policy
- Fraud awareness training
- Risk analysis
- Compliance function

Notes

12: Internal audit

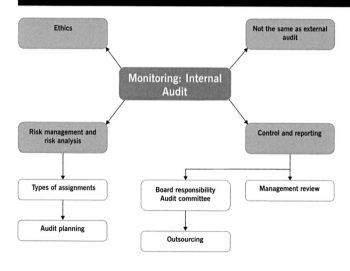

Internal audit

is an independent appraisal function established within an organisation to examine and evaluate its activities as a service to the organisation.

Need for internal audit

Turnbull report (1999, UK) – listed companies without internal audit function should review need annually, and listed companies with internal audit should review annually its scope, authority and resources.

Need for internal audit

- Scale, diversity and complexity
- Number of employees
- Cost-benefit considerations
- Changes in organisational structure
- Changes in key risks
- Internal control problems
- Unexplained/unacceptable events

| Accounting and internal control systems | Financial and operating information | Economy, Efficiency, Effectiveness | Compliance with laws and regulations |

Objectives of internal audit

| Safeguarding of assets | Implementation of organisational objectives | Risk identification and management | Special investigations |

Transaction audits	Time consuming audits of individual transactions, used if systems have broken down or fraud is suspected
Systems audits	Audit of internal controls within the context of a system. Focus on design and operation
Risk-based audits	Assess whether responses to risks adequate, systems and processes robust and mitigate risks
Accounting systems audits	Examine operation of significant controls in major accounting areas
Computer system audits	Test security, accuracy, authorisation and back-up/contingency plan
Operational audits	Designed to confirm adequacy and implementation of control and risk management policies

Value for money audits	Focus on economy, efficiency and effectiveness in the use of resources
Best value audits	Assess whether UK local authorities are achieving continuous improvements by looking at 4Cs: Challenge, Compare, Consult, Compete
Quality audits	Review quality standards and whether actual performance meets quality standards
Management audits	Assessment of effectiveness of management and corporate structure in achievement of objectives and policies
Social audits	Coverage may include health and safety compliance, labour conditions, equal opportunities
Environmental audits	Systematic, documented, periodic and objective evaluation of how well an entity is performing in helping to safeguard the environment

External audit

is a periodic examination of the books of account and records of an entity carried out by an independent third party to ensure that they have been properly maintained, are accurate and comply with established concepts, principles, accounting standards, legal requirements and give a true and fair view of the financial state of the entity.

Distinction between internal and external audit

	Objective	Reporting	Scope	Relationship
Internal audit	Designed to add value and improve an organisation's operations.	Report to management.	Operations of the organisation.	Usually employees of the organisation, although sometimes outsourced.
External audit	Express an opinion on the financial statements.	Report to shareholders.	Financial statements.	Independent of the company and its management. They are appointed by the shareholders.

IIA Standards

Professional proficiency

This includes using staff with sufficient knowledge and experience, compliance with professional standards, proper supervision and due care.

Scope of work

Auditors should assess adequacy of controls, quality of performance, compliance with regulations and standards, asset safeguarding, VFM.

Audit performance

Proper structuring of audit work including planning, examination, reporting and follow-up.

Management

IA should have mission statement, written policies, personnel development, co-ordination with external audit and quality assurance system.

Independence and objectivity

IA should report to audit committee, not finance director and be independent of line management. Auditors should **not** audit their own work.

Outsourcing

Maintaining in-house internal audit function may be expensive and work may not justify employing full-time staff. Many organisations therefore outsource internal audit, possibly to large accountancy firms.

Using same firm to provide external and internal audit services may create independence issues and is forbidden in some jurisdictions (eg America).

Advantages of outsourcing	Disadvantages of outsourcing
☑ Provide quality staff and specialist skills	☒ Irregular monitoring of controls
☑ Assist in developing permanent internal function	☒ Greater expense as supplier makes profit
☑ Staffing and timing flexibility	☒ Frequent changes of staff
☑ More independent than employees	☒ Independence problems if same firm provides internal and external audit
☑ Better at dealing with sensitive areas	

AUDIT PLANNING

Strategic planning

Sets out audit objectives in broad terms including:

- Areas to be covered
- Frequency of coverage
- Resource requirements

Tactical planning

Annual matching of strategic plans to resources and timetables. Includes:

- Programme
- Audit objectives
- Resource allocation
- Contingency allowance

Operational planning

Plan for each individual audit covering:

- Detailed objectives for each area
- Extent of coverage
- Target dates
- Completion arrangements
- Staff responsible

Business risks

are the risks relating to activities carried out within an entity arising from structure, systems, people, products or processes.

Assessment of business risks

Inherent risk

- Relative size of units
- Nature of transactions
- Complexity of operations
- Convertibility of assets
- Computerisation
- Reputation risks

Quality of control (control risk)

- Managerial effectiveness
- Changes in systems
- Changes in personnel
- Rapid growth
- Management pressures
- Time since last review

Risk formula

Risks can then be formally assessed using an **index** that is applied to the areas under consideration to give a ranking.

| Role of internal audit | Internal audit assignments | Internal and external audit | Standards and ethics | Outsourcing | Audit planning and risk analysis | **Audit evidence** |

Sufficiency and appropriateness are **interrelated** & apply to both **tests of control** and **substantive** tests.

ISA 500.6

The auditor shall design and perform audit procedures that are appropriate in the circumstances for the purpose of obtaining sufficient appropriate audit evidence.

Sufficiency
Quantity

Appropriateness
Quality

External evidence (more reliable than internal)
Auditor evidence (collected from auditors better than obtained from entity)
Entity evidence (more reliable if system works well)
Written evidence (more reliable than oral)
Original evidence (original better than photocopies)

Tests of control

The auditors need evidence about two aspects of the system:

- The **design** of the systems (capable of preventing/detecting misstatements?)
- The **operation** of the systems (have they existed/operated properly in the period?)

Audit procedures

- Inspection of assets
- Inspection of documentation
- Observation
- Enquiries
- Confirmation
- Computations
- Analytical procedures

Substantive tests

The auditors are seeking to **substantiate assertions** made by the directors (known as the financial statement assertions).

Financial statement assertions

Existence (an asset or liability exists at the relevant date)

Rights & obligations (asset/liability pertains to the entity at the relevant date)

Occurrence (a transaction/event took place and pertains to the entity)

Completeness (there are no items which are unrecorded or incomplete)

Valuation (asset/liability is recorded at an appropriate carrying value)

Measurement (item is recorded in the correct amount and in the right period)

Presentation/disclosure (law/standards)

Audit sampling

is the application of audit procedures to less than 100% of the items within an account balance or class of transactions such that all sampling units have a chance of selection.

Sample selection

- Random selection
- High value or key terms
- All items over a certain amount
- Items to obtain information about business
- Items to test procedures

Audit sampling and CATS | Analytical review | Internal audit reports | Audit committee and management review

CAATs

are computer-assisted audit techniques, used to test controls, transactions and carry out analytical review.

Audit software

consists of computer programs used by auditors to process data of audit significance from the entity's accounting system.

Test data

is used in conducting audit procedures by entering data, such as a sample of transactions, into an entity's computer system, and comparing the results obtained with predetermined results.

Embedded audit facilities

allow a continuous review of data recorded and treated by system. Audit modules incorporated into enterprise's accounting system.

Analytical review

is an audit technique used to help analyse data to identify trends, errors, fraud, inefficiency and inconsistency. Its purpose is to understand what has happened in a system to compare this with a standard and to identify weaknesses in practice or unusual situations that may require further investigation.

Methods of analytical review

- Ratio analysis
- Non-financial performance analysis
- Internal and external benchmarking
- Trend analysis

Types of analytical procedure

Comparisons can be made with prior period information, anticipated results, predictions, industry information.

Relationships may be between different financial information that is expected to conform to a predicted pattern or between financial and non-financial information.

Ratio analysis

The analysis of relationships between different items of financial data, or financial and non-financial data.

- Comparisons required (previous periods, other companies)
- Calculation on consistent basis
- Correlation between items compared
- Greater detail strengthens analysis
- Ratios distorted by single or unusual items

Trend analysis

Analysis of changes in a given item over time, including period-by-period comparisons, weighted averages, regression analysis.

Reasonableness tests

Development of a prediction for an item based on relationships with other financial or non-financial data, eg comparison with similar firms, comparison with budgets, comparison with other financial information, credibility checks, general business review.

Audit sampling and CAATs	Analytical review	**Internal audit reports**	Audit committee and management review

Recommendations for changes   **Identification of risk and control issues**   **Ensuring action happens**

REPORTING

Contents of report

- Business objectives
- Operational standards
- Risks of current practice
- Control weaknesses

- Causes of weaknesses
- Effects of weaknesses
- Recommendations to solve weaknesses

The audit committee

is a formally constituted committee of an entity's main board of directors whose responsibilities include reviewing internal financial controls, internal control and risk management systems, and monitoring the effectiveness of the internal audit function amongst others.

Benefits of audit committee

- Improve quality of financial reporting
- Create climate of control
- Enable NEDs to play positive role
- Help finance director
- Strengthen position and independence of external auditors
- Increase public confidence

Duties of audit committee

The Cadbury and Smith reports stated that the main duties were:

- **Review of financial statements** including changes in policies, judgemental areas, compliance
- **Relationship with external auditors** including appointment/removal, independence, scope, liaison
- **Review of internal audit** including standards, scope, resources, reporting, work plans, liaison with external auditors, results
- **Review of internal control** including systems adequacy, legal compliance, fraud risk, auditors' reports, disclosures
- **Review of risk management**
- **Investigations**

Review of internal controls

UK's Turnbull committee provided guidance on what board should consider:

- Risk identification/evaluation/management
- Effectiveness of internal control
- Action taken if weaknesses found

When assessing control effectiveness, consider:

- Nature and extent of risks
- Threat risks become reality
- Ability to reduce incidence/impact
- Costs and benefits of controls

Boards should receive reports covering:

- Risk and risk management
- Operation of internal controls
- Actions taken to reduce risks found
- Need for changes in control

Annual review of controls

- Changes in risks/ability to respond
- Management's monitoring of risk and control
- Extent of frequency of reports to board
- Significant controls, failures and weaknesses
- Effectiveness of public reporting

Reporting on risk management

- Acknowledgement of director responsibilities
- System provides reasonable assurance
- How directors have reviewed effectiveness
- Weaknesses leading to material losses

Notes

13: Monitoring

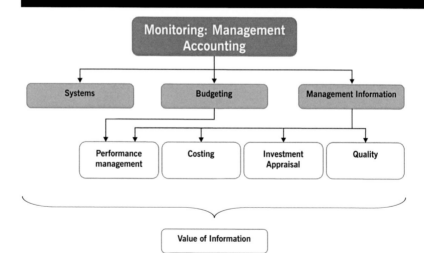

Monitoring: Management Accounting

- Systems
- Budgeting
  - Performance management
  - Costing
  - Investment Appraisal
  - Quality
- Management Information

Value of Information

Management accounting function

Provides information aiding planning, control and decision – making, resource usage and asset security.

Increasing emphasis on linking different sources of information, and providing information tailored to particular decisions, such as risk management.

Measurement of management accounting function

- User satisfaction surveys/complaints
- Delivery of information on time
- Benchmarking v functions in other organisations/external providers
- Speed of query response
- Number of ad hoc reports

Objectives

- Provision of good information
- Provision of value for money service
- Availability of informed personnel
- Flexibility

Strategic management accounting

Stresses factors relating to external parties, customers, competitors. **Forward looking** and concerned with **values**.

Designing a system

- Sources of input and whether sources can deliver required information
- Processing
- Output required based on information needs
- Different types of information (strategic planning, management and operational control)
- Response dependent on detail and how information is presented
- When required

Manufacturing sector performance

- Quality
- Reliability
- Process time
- Flexibility

Service sector performance

- Flexibility
- Innovation
- Resource utilisation
- Excellence
- Financial performance
- Competitiveness

Elements of management accounting systems

Simons identified the need for management accounting systems to be useful for score-keeping, attention-directing and problem-solving. They should assist strategic planning, management control and operational control.

Problems with traditional systems

Recent developments that give traditional systems problems:

- Globalisation and increased competition
- Information technology and data flows
- Reorganisations and mergers

Risks of management accounting systems

1 Excessive emphasis on financial measures

2 Internal orientation

3 Lack of goal congruence

4 Lack of future perspective

5 Failure to adopt the right performance measures

Budget decisions

There are a number of decisions that have to be made in relation to how budgets are prepared:

- Budget centres may be chosen on basis of activities, functions, products, areas, customers
- Focus may be costs, revenues, profit, ROI
- Whether to establish service centres as profit centres, focusing on volume and value of services
- How much managers participate
- Use of beyond budgeting performance targets

Problems with budgeting

- Budgets seen as pressure device
- Budgets of different departments conflict
- Budgetary slack
- Unachievable budgets set
- Efforts limited to achieving targets
- Encourages rigidity
- Excessive concentration on short-term
- Too hard or too soft targets demotivate

Low-level budgeting

Advantages

- ☑ Motivates junior managers
- ☑ Better awareness of management responsibilities
- ☑ Better awareness of detail

Disadvantages

- ☒ Acts against centralisation
- ☒ Managers work in own interests
- ☒ More budget centres, more complexity
- ☒ Greater opportunity for budgetary slack

Timing
Management accountants focus on the production stage, not the design stage when the key decisions are made.

Controllability
Focus is on direct costs, rather than overheads, when overheads are more difficult to control.

Different assets
Systems have difficulty measuring non-tangible assets and how they affect resource allocation and strategic value.

Customers
Systems fail to analyse how customers drive costs.

Cost reporting
Reporting reflects functional structure rather than processes that drive costs and cut across functions.

Absorption costing
Absorption rates based on labour hours are inappropriate for many modern non-labour intensive processes. Activity-based costing may be a better method.

Standard costing	Inappropriate where flexibility/customisation/service are important.
Short-term financial measures	Take too long to produce/too narrow.
Cost accounting methods	Emphasis on quantifiable financial benefits at expense of non-quantifiable or non-financial benefits.
Variances	Can produce inappropriate responses (excess inventory).
Investment appraisal	Fail to consider financial constraints/strategic issues.
Transfer pricing	Problems resolving conflict between economic price and inappropriate behaviour transfer price may encourage.
Balanced scorecard	Range of measures, links with strategy, but difficult to understand/gain overall impression.
Environmental reporting	Full cost accounting including hidden costs, contingent liabilities, rectification costs.

Just in time/Total Quality Management

Both emphasise commitment to continuous improvement. JIT involves search for excellence in design + operation of production management. TQM applies zero defects philosophy to management of all resources and relationships, and focuses on customers.

Life cycle costing

Majority of product's life cycle costs committed at early stages of cycle and hence highest cost controls are required at this stage.

Focus on planning and control of life cycle, and spending commitments in early years.

Throughput accounting

Identification and elimination of bottleneck resources by overtime, product changes and process alterations to reduce set-up and waiting times.

Lean management accounting

Lean management accounting aims to support production flow based on customer demand. It is designed to encourage continuous quality improvement and the elimination of waste. It uses management through value streams and target costing to eliminate distortions that result in non-optimal behaviour.

Target costing

Product is developed, managers determine market selling price and desired profit margin. Cost of production is therefore the balancing figure which must be achieved.

Kaizen

Kaizen is applied during the production process. It focuses on key elements of operations, production, purchasing and distribution. Aims to achieve a specified cost reduction through continuous improvements, rather than one-off changes.

Transaction cost economics

Relevant for determining transfer prices. Focuses on costs such as negotiation, administration, time commitments and obligations.

Backflush costing

Can significantly reduce detailed work done by accounting department. Costs calculated and charged when product sold or when transferred to finished goods store.

14: Control and direction

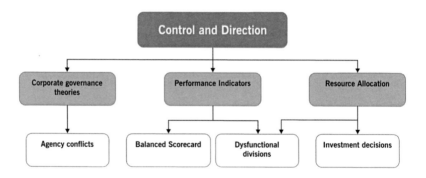

Ideally **performance measures** should reward behaviour that maximises the corporate good (in both long term and short term). But:

- Management/staff will concentrate only upon what they know is being measured.
- Good performance that satisfies management's/staff's own sense of what is important will not necessary work towards the corporate good (problem of **goal congruence**).

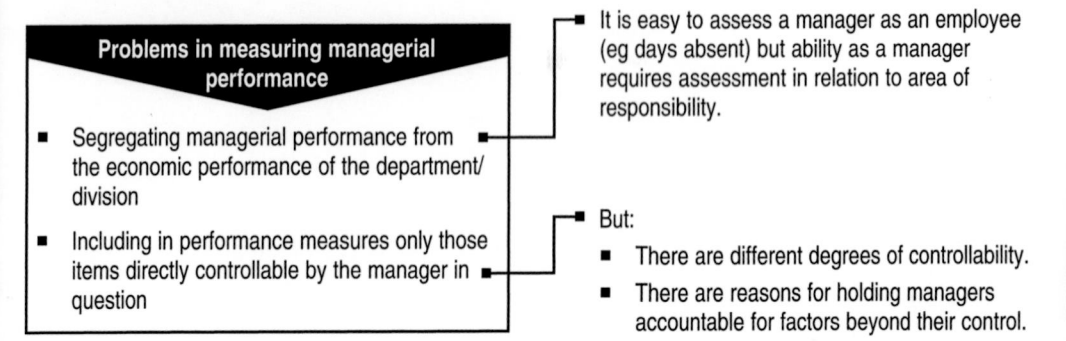

Problems in measuring managerial performance

- Segregating managerial performance from the economic performance of the department/ division

- Including in performance measures only those items directly controllable by the manager in question

- It is easy to assess a manager as an employee (eg days absent) but ability as a manager requires assessment in relation to area of responsibility.

- But:
  - There are different degrees of controllability.
  - There are reasons for holding managers accountable for factors beyond their control.

| Reward management | Accountability | Benefits and problems | Reward schemes | Investments and projects | Feasibility study | Project control |

Accountability

1. **Hard accountability** (financial and quantitative information) which covers three areas
   - Counting (converting activities and outcomes into numbers)
   - Ensuring that numbers are accounted for (how and why an outcome occurred)
   - Being held accountable (for accounting and for the underlying circumstances)
2. **Soft accountability** (the human impact on the system and its role in shaping, evaluating and implementing goals)

Steps to accountability

1. Choose and publicise accepted performance measures
2. Identify the benefits of the measures
3. Identify and understand problems in their use
4. Consider how to counter perceived problems

Accountability and controls

Three broad categories of control mechanisms:

1. Action (or behavioural) control
2. Personnel and cultural control
3. Results (or output) control

Benefits of performance measures

- Clarify organisational objectives
- Develop agreed measures of activity
- Greater understanding of processes
- Facilitate comparison of the performance of different organisations
- Facilitate target setting (for the organisation and managers)
- Promote accountability of the organisation to its stakeholders

These problems highlight the issue of congruence between the goals of individuals and the goals of the organisation.

Problems of performance measurement

- **Tunnel vision** – measure customer satisfaction
- **Sub-optimisation** – quantify all objectives
- **Myopia** – a long-term perspective among staff
- **Measure fixation** – constant review of the performance measurement system
- **Misrepresentation** – flexible use of measures
- **Misinterpretation** – audit of data used
- **Gaming** – involvement of staff at all levels
- **Ossification** – constant review of performance measurement system

Benefits of linking reward schemes and performance

- Provides an incentive to achieve good performance
- Attracts and keeps valuable employees
- Use of share schemes motivates managers to act in the organisation's long-term interests (increase market value)
- Creates an organisation focused on continuous improvement
- Makes employees aware of what creates organisational success

Problems associated with reward schemes

- Encourage dysfunctional behaviour
- Schemes to combat short-termism may not motivate
- Employees will concentrate on what is measured
- Higher output achieved at the expense of quality
- Undervalue intrinsic rewards
- Lack of goal congruence

14: Control and direction

Stages of new development

Initial assessment

▼

Business analysis

▼

Product design

▼

Early testing

▼

Final testing

▼

Product launch

Reasons for new product development

- Changing needs of customers (adequate demand)
- Competitive advantage
- Environmental threats and opportunities
- Extend/refresh the product portfolio
- Extend product life

Project phases

1 Initiation ⎫
2 Formation ⎬ Defining
3 Objective setting ⎭

4 Task planning ⎫
5 Feasibility ⎪
6 Fact finding ⎪
7 Position analysis ⎬ Planning
8 Options generation ⎪
9 Options evaluation ⎭

10 Design and development ⎫
11 Implementation ⎬ Implementing

12 Review ⎫
13 Completion ⎬ Controlling and completing

Project success factors

- Clearly defined mission and goals
- Top management support
- Competent project manager
- Competent team members
- Sufficient resources
- Excellent communication channels
- Clear client focus

FEASIBILITY STUDY

Operational → **Technical** → **Social** → **Ecological** → **Economic**

Feasibility study team

Team should have clear terms of reference and be drawn from the departments affected by the investments. All team members should be able to be objectively critical, and at least some should be able to assess technical and organisational implications of the proposals.

Option evaluation

Stage 1.	Create base constraints
Stage 2.	Create option outlines
Stage 3.	Assess impact on operations of relevant department/organisations
Stage 4.	Review proposals with people affected

Project control – key elements

- **Organisation** – Terms of reference defining objectives, timescales, roles and resources
- **Reporting structure**
- **Overall project plan** supplemented by subsidiary plans and budgets
- **Quality standards**
- **Risk assessment** and **management**
- **Reports on progress**
- **Dealing with problems and slippage** may involve rescheduling. Implications of major changes should be carefully investigated
- **Reviewing investment success** including whether performance good or bad, purpose(s), quantitative and qualitative measures

Post-completion audit

is an objective and independent appraisal of the success of a capital project in progressing the business.

- Incentive for managers to consider benefits/costs
- Indicates efficiency improvements
- Identifies good/poor performers
- Identifies weaknesses in forecasting

Problems with post-audits

- ☒ Number of uncontrollable factors
- ☒ Difficult to identify costs/benefits
- ☒ Costly and time-consuming
- ☒ Managers become too risk-averse

Notes

Notes

Notes

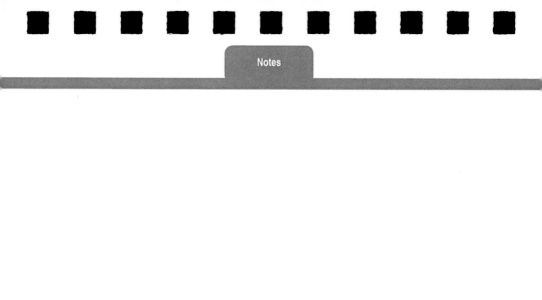

Notes

Notes

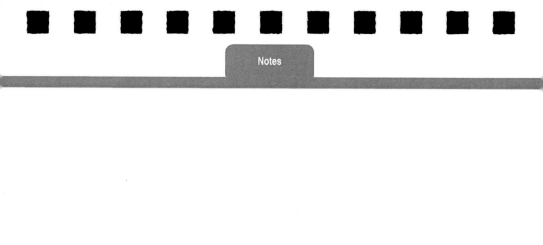

Notes

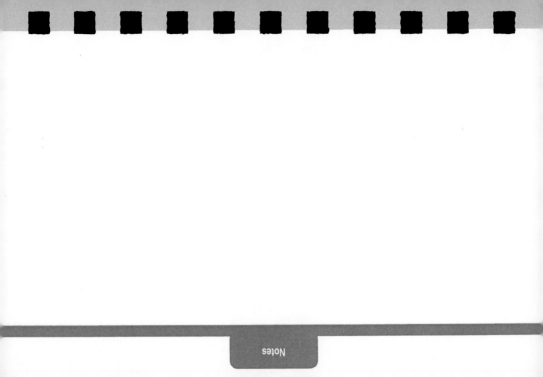

Notes

Notes

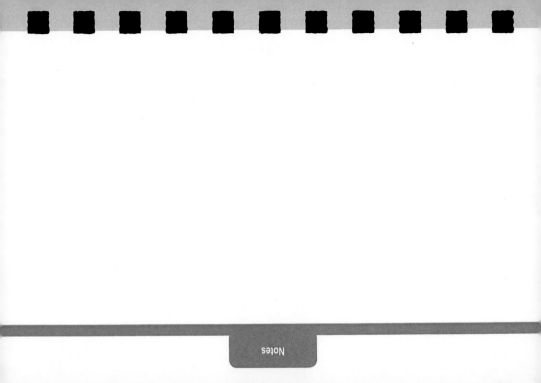

Notes

Notes

Notes

Notes